country
home

Andreas von Einsiedel
Johanna Thornycroft

country
home

MERRELL
LONDON · NEW YORK

Country style, in all its national variations, has enormous universal appeal. The country idyll is part romantic dream based on nostalgia and perhaps an innate sense of the rural past, and part desire for cosseting comfort. Open fires, heavy drapes, eiderdowns on beds, and sofas softened with plaid or Welsh blankets are part of a traditional melange of country living, but this most English of styles is popular everywhere. Evolved through practical necessity every country has its own signature look, but much mixing and matching goes on internationally: the particular charms of French, Swedish and English styles especially have been absorbed and adapted worldwide.

It is unsurprising that country style has influenced interior design more than any other. Traditionally, country homes, apart from the grandest, were generally less about show and all about what was locally available, practical and affordable – and what would be domestic and welcoming. The term eclectic, now used so freely, is still the best way to describe cottage, farm or manor house rooms with their charming muddle of recycled fabrics, old furniture, mismatched china and glass and, until recently, the minimal use of technology.

The desire for country style lives on, comes to town, retreats according to fashion, but always returns. One's own idea of country decoration is likely to determine whether a modern hob is inserted into the top of an old coal-burning range, or whether a brand new kitchen includes a Belfast sink, reclaimed cupboards and a ceiling-mounted clothes pulley even though dishwashers, tumble dryers and central heating render many country items redundant. The point is that they are still practical and appear comforting, old-fashioned and friendly, and appeal, in a real or imagined way, to our desire for a slower and quieter way of life.

Country style generally includes plenty of craftsmanship and nearly always relies on antique furniture to create atmosphere. After all, country people tended to live by a 'make-do-and-mend' philosophy, so that the layers and additions of many generations are retained and added to rather than being abandoned for the sake of a makeover. The houses shown in this book are both large and small, architecturally diverse and international; some are particularly glamorous, but they all contain the essential ingredients of comfort, colour and pattern. Those in warm climates do not rely on layers of rugs or heavy curtains to achieve the look, but even here the mix of old and new combines to

produce a style that is relaxed and confident. For millions of city dwellers a country house is the best antidote to fast-paced modern living, while the desire for a house with a garden or some land is nothing new.

One of the most delightful aspects of the continuous reinterpretation of country style is the sheer variety of furniture, textiles, china, lighting and finishes available. Imagination is the only limit to individual originality and creativity. French fruitwood is perennially popular, as are painted pieces from Scandinavia, France, Italy and eastern Europe. English oak endures, especially early twentieth-century Arts and Crafts designs. Anglo-Indian and Asian antiques mix with rush-seated chairs and pewter candlesticks. Worn Oriental carpets or modern striped and checked rugs work well with simple or elaborately sophisticated furniture, but no country house looks entirely comfortable with fitted carpets except, perhaps, in a bedroom. Larger country houses evolve and take one on something of a Grand Tour, either within a single region or worldwide. One tends to have more of everything in the country. Certainly books and magazines abound, but so do colours and patterns (even a contemporary take on country style will include textiles or wallpaper that would be banished in the city). People feel less restrained about their choices in the country, where quality matters less than rusticity, comfort or relaxation, and where priority is given to family, leisure and entertaining. As anyone with a wonderful country house knows, friends vie for weekend invitations. Country house hotel owners long for their guests to admire their decoration as that of a private house. The great houses of England and Europe draw millions of visitors, all hoping to experience something of life in the 'big house', to admire the graciously furnished rooms, the servants' quarters and kitchens, the dairy and stables. We muse over rows of shiny copper pans, washboards, oil lamps and the accoutrements of those far-off times, and try to create a similar look for ourselves.

If the detail of country style varies from nation to nation, the essence of country style is universally consistent in looking back in time rather than forward. Forgotten are the hardships of isolation, growing one's own food, and the discomfort of excessive cold or heat before the advent of central heating and air conditioning. Patina is prized, faded is good, worn is better, and nostalgia for our rural past continues to inform country style.

French polish

That rarefied part of Provence known as the 'Golden Triangle' (between Avignon, Arles and Aix-en-Provence) is filled with exceptionally beautiful homes, many with large, superbly designed gardens, of which this is a perfect example. Their owners come from Paris, Northern Europe, the United States and beyond. Rarely are the farmhouses, or 'mas' as they are known, in good enough condition to satisfy the desires of the new owners. Specialist firms in the region, with intimate knowledge of restoration techniques, now bring back to life many of the semi-ruined mas and bastides. Usually built of local limestone, they were originally the houses and barns that formed the hub of local farming communities, and the best restoration programmes make use of traditional methods and materials. Attached barns become drawing-rooms, tractor sheds make orangeries, and often a new staircase has to be built to reach the upper floors. So skilful is much of the work that it is barely possible to tell what is original and what is new. Window glass appears old, floor- and wall-tiles are reclaimed and carefully selected for patina, fireplace surrounds are bought second-hand from dealers, and walls are finished in traditional colours. It is a style that is much copied throughout the world but is never quite as good as the real thing.

Dowager duchess

The old stone Dower House in north-east England was in urgent need of sympathy and restoration when the current owners came across it. Originally Elizabethan, it was rebuilt in 1801, but much of its character had been lost after generations of remodelling and partitioning. To create the perfect family home takes courage, talent and the knowledge that so much of the expenditure will be unseen, hidden in walls, roof-space and under floors, as the massive job of installing new plumbing and cabling is carried out. The designer–owner had done it all before, and fortunately all the furniture from the old house fitted perfectly. The ground-floor kitchen and dining-room had been a separate flat, and once it had been gutted, the owner went to Chalon in London for a new country-style kitchen to complement the large Aga cooker. The first-floor bedrooms and bathrooms are warm but pale. The expansive living areas on the ground floor are richer in detail and colour than those above, employing silks and suede, needlepoint and linen. The design is a triumph of function and country-house comfort.

25

Village life

Near the Cabo de Creus, an hour's drive north of Barcelona, is the fishing village of Cadaques. The young couple who bought this old house were holidaying from France and decided it was the ideal place to return to. The most appealing aspect of the house was the way in which it was built into the hillside. It required no structural work, but all the services were renewed, and they were left with a blank canvas on which to add colour and texture. Grey, blue, green and yellow colour washes were applied, and previous layers of paint were scraped back to expose past colour-schemes in their mottled variations. As it is a summer holiday home furnishings were kept simple and inexpensive. Trestle tables, cotton ticking fabrics and market finds from all over Europe fit perfectly into the pretty, rustic interior. As there are no windows at the back of the house, it is cool and dimly lit – the perfect hot-weather retreat.

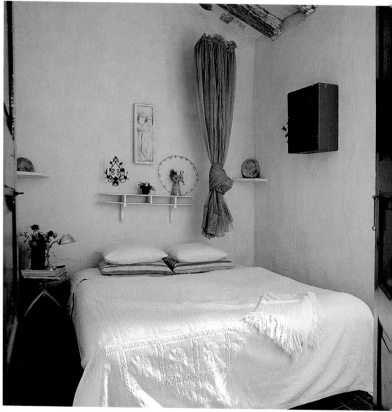

Anglo-American

Warm climates demand architecture that allows a house and garden to be far more accessible to each another than is common in Northern Europe. Open verandas, perhaps slatted shutters to admit fresh air, and plenty of glazed doors are the norm, allowing the house to be opened up from back to front in the hot summer months. The interiors, though, can range from seaside resort to cosy country, and here an English owner asked a local designer to interpret an Anglo-American approach to a new house, set in idyllic surroundings on a lake in Georgia. It is a rich mix of antique, reproduction and contemporary furniture, textured fabrics, patterns and colour. Some corners of the house are definitely English in style; there is French country as well as American Federal furniture; and there are pieces of Oriental blue-and-white porcelain. Chairs and tables are set out on the wrap-around verandas, with the walls lined in white-painted clapboard. Tall trees set in trim green lawns shade parts of the house, and the views over the water are sensational.

47

Chartreuse charm

Unusually, the garden of this fine and much-loved seventeenth- and eighteenth-century hunting-lodge in Périgord, south-west France, was laid out and replanted before the old internal partitions were stripped out to reveal the bones of the house. Unlike the garden, which is filled with roses and lush herbaceous planting, the house has a sparseness that its owner attributes, in part at least, to five years spent living in Japan. The walls are mostly a soft yellow, the floors are bare poplar boards, tiles or stone flags, and there are no curtains and few paintings. The walls are hung instead with groups of prints and drawings, some by Chardin and Henry Moore. Internal shutters control light, and even on a dull day the house glows with a gentle warmth. In the grand salon a pair of bookcases stand either side of the chimney-piece, and a Regency panel above it displays prints. Much of the French furniture is painted, and in the petit salon, red fabric from Mali covers the sofa while two Louis XVI chairs are in a fabric by Le Manach. English rush matting covers the floor. The bathrooms feature old-fashioned claw-foot baths and Pierre Frey fabric lining the cupboards. The chestnut beamed tower room, formerly a tobacco-drying barn, was opened up for use as a bedroom.

Country classic

The English country house was, and still is, an important inspiration for many international designers, but there is nothing quite like the real thing. Formed of a central block built in 1680 and a 1720 extension of identical wings on either side, this ochre-washed brick house has barely changed since it was completed. Minor alterations were made to the interiors in the late twentieth century: the kitchen floor was raised, a warren of service rooms behind the rear staircase was opened up to become an informal sitting-room, and glass doors were added to the dining-room, giving access to a garden terrace. Several bedrooms became bathrooms, fitted out in period style with deep free-standing baths and plenty of large cupboards. The old wide-plank floors and staircases are original, and the decoration is pure country classic, relying on collections of textiles, antique furniture, mirrors, porcelain, and faded Oriental rugs, creating the impression of generations of occupation by the same family. The walls and panelling are painted in off-whites to balance the patterns, colours and textures of contemporary and antique textiles used for curtains and upholstery.

Northern light

Set in rural East Anglia in the east of England, a group of three thatched cottages was converted into one dwelling by its Danish owner. The interiors of the house, and particularly the studio, reflect his love of all things Scandinavian, especially that luminous, soft grey-white that works so well in northern climates. He has not slavishly relied on Danish and Swedish pieces, but the overall impression is that of a country house in Sweden where French influences in the eighteenth and nineteenth centuries made quite an impact. The house and studio share the same calm and airy aesthetic, a monochrome world but one that is constantly changing with the seasons and varying levels of light. Floorboards, beams and panelled walls are all washed in the same colour; mirrors, chairs, a secrétaire and chest are similarly pale. There is little pattern to disturb the serenity – just a checked fabric used on a sofa and chairs, plain gunmetal grey here and there, and a floral stripe on a bedroom chair. Touches of silver, black and gilt punctuate the pale spaces, contrasting beautifully with the quiet grey wash.

74

Far pavilion

This gem of a miniature pavilion is one of a pair, set close to the stone boundary walls of a Provençal estate that includes a restored eighteenth-century hunting-lodge. Tiny but perfect in its proportions and detailing, it provides a quiet country retreat for a man who works in the frenetic world of international architecture and design. The pavilion contains few rooms – an entrance-hall, salon and conservatory-like kitchen on the ground floor, and two bedrooms and a bathroom on the first, both levels connected by a mahogany spiral staircase – but it nonetheless feels rather special. The setting is sublime and so is the classic French interior. The walls are completely covered in La Toile Villageoise of an old design in madder and cream, which has rapidly become antique in appearance from the open fire. Tall mirror-panelled cupboards are painted black, as is the specially made kitchen shelving. Black brings weight and balance to many interiors, effective here in the white-walled, glass-roofed kitchen. Apart from the piano, brought from the United States, all the contents are French, and most date from the eighteenth and nineteenth centuries, except the charming 1950s Jansen tole table with a tree-trunk base adorned with suitable wildlife.

Coastal heritage

Everything about the interior of this house suits its remarkable location on England's Dorset coast, an area that was declared a World Heritage Site in 2002. The house, one of a pair, was built in the 1880s as a holiday home. The current owner, a designer, had dreamed of a seaside home for years and had rented cottages near by for some time but never expected she would find the right property as easily as she did. It had been a guesthouse for many years and required a formidable amount of work to upgrade the entire building. The former double garage became a very large kitchen/dining-room, designed to have the best possible views of the sea. The front-facing wall is entirely glass; the owner enclosed the large terrace across the façade but allowed for plenty of windows, one of which is framed by a weathered teak door frame. All the paintwork was bought or mixed to echo the colours of the local cliffs and fossils, and old pallets, driftwood and scaffolding have become shelves and cupboards. Although the scene is undoubtedly English, this interesting house has a colonial ambience about it that is relaxed, airy and supremely comfortable.

90

Tuscan belle

Set four-square in the rich agricultural lands of eastern Tuscany, this eighteenth-century farmhouse has been restored by a Belgian artist and designer to become a multi-family holiday home. The house had been uninhabited for years and was almost derelict. A two-year restoration programme was undertaken in which careful preservation was the main objective. A loggia runs across the front, facing fields and a range of blue-green hills in the distance. The ground floor, formerly cattle barns, houses a large kitchen, a bedroom off the hallway and, down one side, an exotic 'Turquerie' that has been created with hand-painted fabrics and wall decorations. An enormous fireplace dominates the first floor, which would originally have been the kitchen. Now the room is used as a sitting-room, which is cool in summer and warm in winter. There are numerous bedrooms, each one differently but simply decorated in faded soft colours. All bathrooms are the same, varying only in shape and size. The designer and her architect worked in complete accord, one complementing the other, and at the project's completion nothing appears to be new and intervention seems minimal.

101

Cotswold country

The acquisition of a country house is often a tale of falling in love, not something that was difficult in this case, as the location in the Windrush Valley, a short distance from Oxford, is one of the most sought-after in England. The farmhouse, originally a pair of late fifteenth-century cottages, had been enlarged in all directions over the centuries. In the late 1990s it had settled as a rather tired Georgian creation, not without charm, but barely suited to its owner's international lifestyle and business. After a period of getting a feel for the house and its many outbuildings, she asked a local architect, a specialist in heritage work and the local vernacular, to advise on what would become a major transformation. Taking the seventeenth century and the Arts and Crafts movement as their base, they spent four years designing, altering and creating the manor house you can see today. One important factor was the fact that the house should age well. Lime plaster, sawn green oak and reclaimed flagstones immediately changed the interior, along with the sensitive removal of walls, allowing a better use of space. Small rooms and passages were swept away, windows enlarged or lowered, and a brand new bedroom wing was added. Opulent fabrics, Asian furniture and specially commissioned furniture combine to create an unusually stylish interior.

Rescue and revival

It takes imagination and courage to turn a run-down group of Provençal buildings into a dream home, let alone find them in the first place, given the popularity of Provence as an international holiday destination where ownership is prized above renting. From the start the owner could visualize renovating this mid-1850s house, which is at the edge of a village, to fulfil her desire for open-plan summer and winter living. The kitchen and expansive ground-floor reception rooms were created by removing part of the existing stone dividing walls and inserting broad arches instead. Right across the front, French doors can be opened to blur the boundary between the inside and the full-width limestone terrace. The house contained some welcome secrets, revealed only after generations of plasterboard had been stripped out: wonderfully distressed beams, a grand fireplace and distinctive stonework indicated that the original builder was a man of some means. A major element of the works included building the interior of the barn, which now houses the master bedroom. The garden, formerly just a car park, has been transformed, and now at its centre is an enormous black swimming-pool, edged in stone and surrounded by fruit trees, roses, clematis and a wall of bamboo.

123

Cornish cream

Located on the Cornish coast, close to the sea in south-west England, this 1960s house was turned into a much-loved family holiday home by the managing director of an international fabrics house. After replacing doors and removing all reminders of the 1960s, it seemed natural to follow both an American and an English tradition of using tongue-and-groove boarding and stripped and sanded floorboards as a starting point. Although traditional in feel, the use of pale colours, little pattern and functional furniture in simple shapes has established a classic summer look that is airy and light but warm in winter. A deep sofa and comfortable chairs in the main sitting-room are the only really large pieces. An antique chair, painted wooden chairs and cane chairs all look relaxed and casual, and blue has been effectively used, in stripes, checks and solid colour, as an appropriate seaside accent. Naturally the owner loves fabrics, and various linens and cottons have been used throughout the house. Curtains are casually looped up at the corners or left unlined to let in light and fresh air. The stairs have been painted in two tones to emulate a carpet runner but bare boards are the norm. Relaxed and friendly, this is an ideal holiday home.

Another country

Approached along a narrow country road, with a barren rocky ridge on one side and flat expansive farmland on the other, this grand bastide sits raised on a broad terrace, seemingly untouched for centuries. All is not what it seems, but so sensitive was the expert restoration of this range of Provençal barns that it is hard to imagine that this house was recently a ruin. The owners are American, the wife an interior designer who might have been an acolyte of Madame de Pompadour, such is her love of eighteenth-century French design and decoration. The architectural firm that carried out the work is renowned for their knowledge of period detail and ability to source the correct materials, be they fireplaces or window glass. While many of the rooms are filled with superb pieces from the period, this is a relaxed family home with numerous guest bedrooms, great entertaining spaces and intimate private quarters. Matt-grey and milky-white paintwork sets off collections of early Gien faïence, old oil paintings, Provençal fruitwood furniture and elaborate gilt frames. Many of the contents were bought locally, while fabrics came from Pierre Frey in Paris or from the United States. Highly detailed planning and the expertise of both owner and architect have created an exceptional family home, imbued with history and great presence.

Crown jewel

An ancient house with royal connections and land has for centuries been something to which the English aspire. Often much reduced in size or, in the case of smaller houses, added to over the centuries, owners have to make numerous tough decisions about the future of such properties. This house bankrupted its builder in the sixteenth century, and later much of the enormous building was demolished. Even so, a sizeable portion remained, which was again extended in the 1800s. It has been owned by the same family ever since. The current family recognizes and enjoys the ups and downs of living in a historic house, including the fact that today such a house and garden have to pay their own way. Restoration is a constant consideration, with much of the investment going unseen into roof repairs or renewing electrical systems, but a great deal of the extraordinary charm of old houses lies in the many surviving layers of previous generations' pictures, furniture and fabrics. Bathrooms and kitchens have been updated but in an old-fashioned style, and while the house is a busy family home there is a palpable sense of history in every room. It takes great skill and energy to keep such a house so fresh and alive.

148

Summer hideaway

Major renovation or almost total rebuilding is sometimes required to bring a house up to date and back to life. With a principal residence in Switzerland, the owners of this house near Nice, in the South of France, had spent many happy holidays here but they decided it needed to be redesigned. A London-based design duo was asked to come up with plans. There were a number of problems associated with the 1930s stone building, and after much discussion it was agreed that the property would be rebuilt. It needed to be enlarged where possible, and a local architect–builder was called in to advise on construction and the supply of correct materials. In order to retain a strong country character, many of the stone walls were left in their natural state; others were just painted, while in some rooms they were both plastered and painted. Structural beams were exposed and the window frames left natural. Outdoor living is an essential part of any holiday home and in France it is usual to create several shady dining areas, but here cooler evenings have been catered for by building an open-sided pool-house, complete with fireplace. The interiors are furnished with a mix of contemporary and antique furniture and made cosy by the many warm-toned timbers used throughout the house.

Modern Mallorca

Although Mallorca has become an increasingly busy tourist destination and favoured location for holiday homes, it takes only a step back from the coastline to realize that the island still has numerous old farmhouses for sale and some very special sites on which to build. A couple who once bought and restored a house here, originally as a holiday home, quickly made it their permanent base, and developed a thriving building, restoration and design business, catering to busy Europeans who need a reliable and knowledgeable team to create their own dream homes. The owner of this house was a client of theirs who favoured a new house in the country with plenty of shady seating areas, a pool and good-sized casual entertaining spaces, but the open site required a great deal of landscaping before building could begin. The use of architectural salvage and recycled materials plays an important part in the team's designs, providing new houses with a feeling of age and atmosphere. Furniture and fittings are from a wide range of sources, chosen for comfort or patina, shape or suitability. Both architect and designer have created a superb house with more than a nod to the vernacular, and it looks absolutely right in its dramatic island setting.

Decorative sympathy

Acquiring a country house or cottage is an enduring and romantic dream for many people. Set in a forest, a converted barn or an old stable block – the setting and original purpose of the property doesn't seem to matter as long as it is in the countryside, but such a home is difficult to find in many countries. The owner of this two-hundred-year-old north German cottage is well aware of its rarity value. Found through word of mouth and previously owned by a couple who had the same decorative sympathies, little work was required to create exactly what the new owner wanted from her weekend and holiday retreat. The roof was re-thatched, a shower-room added and the whole place painted in the pale colours that reflect its location near the Danish border. Paint has transformed not only the interior but also most of the furniture: bought for shape and function, regardless of condition, it is all painted in the Scandinavian colours so beloved of its artistic châtelaine. This cottage has it all: a quiet agricultural location, sweeping views, a large pond and a garden that is developing into a cottage classic.

Perfect Provence

To many Parisians, and an international band of Francophiles, the Luberon and the area around St-Remy-de-Provence are some of the most coveted places in France in which to own a house. Apart from the climate, the views and the wonderful food and wine, there are first-class restorers, designers and craftsmen who can completely transform old farmhouses and manors to suit discriminating owners. This house is a superb example of a major architectural and design collaboration. Virtually everything was replaced, but with great sensitivity to proportion and period detail, and extensive use has been made of reclaimed materials – from floor-tiles and chimney-pieces to beams and doors. New stonework is supplied from quarries that have been in use for millennia. The interior decoration was carried out by a friend of the owners who owns a wonderful house near by, is well versed in French style and who knows the best sources for fabrics and furniture. Relying largely on white, cream and pale grey, she has created a cool and utterly restful interior of great comfort and style.

190

Highland fling

Very few people actually buy castles, but this magnificent sixteenth-century colossus on the edge of the Firth of Moray in Scotland was found and restored by a man who, since childhood, had dreamed of owning and restoring such a place. Although bought as a ruin, it was nonetheless a late medieval Z-plan tower. Armed with little money but plenty of knowledge and lots of enthusiasm, the owners began a seven-year restoration programme. It was a labour of love: eighty-six windows and doors were made by local craftsmen; the correct timber, slate and stone had to be found; and, keen to avoid using any wrong materials, they mixed the lime and pigments for the exterior finish themselves. Fortunately, the owners' textile and carpet business manufactures designs with a Scottish history and palette, and they were able to use a great many of their own products throughout the interior. Some of the furniture was made at the castle and other pieces were inherited or bought locally. The walls are clad with either wooden planks or softly painted plaster, the windows are curtainless, but the beds and sofas are draped and warmed with hangings, blankets and woollen fabrics. An enormous challenge, this is a dream come true.

French leave

A charming nineteenth-century house in the Marne valley in France is where a well-known New Zealand artist lives and works, in a setting that is not so very different from her rural homeland. Admittedly, though, nobody in the Antipodes built houses like this – a charming bourgeois brick-and-stone mini château with numerous tall timber-framed windows screened by grey-blue painted shutters. Described as a ruin inside when bought, the interiors nonetheless still contained typical terracotta floor-tiles, old exposed beams and some cupboards, but within the restored shell a quirky mix of partitions has been added, designed to fulfil the owner's very specific requirements. Fitted within the formerly empty first floor is a plywood structure that divides the space into a bedroom, a sizeable library, a bathroom and an office. Much creative work has gone into enlivening the tired old rooms: paintings, of course, but also collections both decorative and unusual abound. The garden is a constant source of joy and produce, while the house provides an inspirational backdrop to artistic endeavour.

204

Georgian tradition

Set on rising ground within park-like gardens, this late Georgian house in mid-Wales was not in good repair when its owners first saw it, but the location, the views and the complete lack of neighbours convinced them that it could easily become a dream home. Architecture of this period is, of course, much sought-after. Room sizes and their number are usually good, often allowing generous en-suite bathrooms; window proportions have never been bettered; staircases are often top-lit; and, if luck would have it, a number of good marble fireplace surrounds will have survived. The owner is a London art dealer who specializes in British paintings, and his wife is an interior designer, so there was never any doubt that the refurbishment and decoration of their fairly large country house would be anything but a superb example of the genre. Naturally there are many wonderful works of art here, ranging from large equestrian canvases to small portraits. A warren of utility rooms became an adjoining kitchen and breakfast-room, French in style with doors leading to the garden. All the bedrooms are furnished in the best country-house tradition of gentle colour, comfort and warmth.

Entente cordiale

The owners of this estate near Le Mans in France have combined their possessions and style with great accord. The wife, an English interior designer, and her French husband took on the 1806 Directoire property immediately after their marriage. A pretty two-storey house with numerous guest bedrooms, some of which are set behind dormer windows in the roof, it has the classic, highly desirable proportions of the period. A broad, raised stone terrace graces the front, while in the centre is a double entrance-hall, the staircase rising from a smaller hall behind. To the left is a large reception room, and beyond it another, used for shooting parties, runs the full depth of the house. Reached by way of a bright corridor is the dining-room, and beyond that a large library, which links to the kitchen. The decoration throughout relies on a mix of wonderful antique furniture and English and French textiles. There is an old walled farmyard behind the house, and ponds, woods and fields surround the property, creating a private haven of peace and quiet.

223

225

Traditional spirit

There are numerous difficult decisions to make during the restoration of an old house. The balance between retaining the character and patina of age, while bringing services and the flow of space up to date, can be a daunting task, and the owners of this Mallorcan house called in a respected designer to pull the project together. The house was a ruin but, by taking great care to use local materials and finishes, they have created a home of great charm that is suitable for both a modern lifestyle and the sunny island setting. Floor finishes vary widely from terracotta to pebble and tile. The interiors are relaxed, light and airy, using shades of white, cream and soft blue and green; beams are bleached or left in their natural wood tones. The furniture, most of which is antique European, is either painted or waxed wood and the choice of fabrics is summery and pale. Taking the view that they wanted neither a town or country look the owners have mixed up the contents in a relaxed manner, enlivening the pale scheme with touches of vivid red, blue or black.

Credits

ages 228–37
Interior: Holga Stewen Interior
Design
Architecture: Fritz Hauri
Feature originally sourced and
produced by Victoria Ahmadi.

Acknowledgements

Andreas von Einsiedel would
like to thank warmly the many
owners, designers and
architects featured in this
book.

Biographies

Andreas von Einsiedel
has specialized in interiors
photography for the past
twenty years. Based in
London, he works
internationally, and is
particularly known for his work
using only naturally available
light. He is a regular
contributor to the *World of
Interiors*, *House & Garden*,
Architectural Digest and other
titles in the United States,
Australia and Europe. He has
photographed subjects for
over twenty books.

Johanna Thornycroft
is a freelance writer and
journalist who regularly
contributes design features
to newspapers and interiors
magazines worldwide. She has
travelled extensively and spent
long periods living in Africa
and the Middle East. She is the
author of several books,
including *The Provençal House*
(2003), *The Russian House*
(2005) and *Dream Homes*
(Merrell, 2005), all with
photography by Andreas
von Einsiedel.

First published 2006 by Merrell Publishers Limited

Head office
81 Southwark Street
London SE1 0HX

New York office
49 West 24th Street, 8th Floor
New York, NY 10010

merrellpublishers.com

Photography copyright © 2006 Andreas von Einsiedel
Text, design and layout copyright © 2006 Merrell
Publishers Limited

Publisher Hugh Merrell
Editorial Director Julian Honer
US Director Joan Brookbank
Sales and Marketing Manager Kim Cope
Sales and Marketing Executive Sarah Unitt
Sales and Marketing Assistant Nicola Davies
US Sales and Marketing Assistant Elizabeth Choi
Managing Editor Anthea Snow
Project Editors Claire Chandler, Rosanna Fairhead
Editor Helen Miles
Art Director Nicola Bailey
Designer Paul Shinn
Production Manager Michelle Draycott
Production Controller Sadie Butler

British Library Cataloguing-in-Publication Data:
Einsiedel, Andreas von
Country home. – (Inspirations)
1.Interior decoration 2.Interior decoration –
Pictorial works 3.Country homes 4.Country homes –
Pictorial works
I.Title II.Thornycroft, Johanna
747'.091734

ISBN 1 85894 357 4

Produced by Merrell Publishers
Designed by Martin Lovelock
Printed and bound in China